TIME TO DECIDE

A CAREER & BUSINESS CHOICE MANUAL

CHIGBO UGWUOKE

FOUNDER OF THE INSTITUTE FOR CAREER & CHARACTER DEVELOPMENT,
ABUJA, NIGERIA

Goforthebest International Ltd, London, UK

*Dedicated to my wife Ugochi,
my boy Chibunkem and the entire Ugwuoke family.*

ACKNOWLEDGEMENTS

I am most grateful to my lovely wife Ugochi and my son Chibunkem who both had a taste of the fate of a writer's family. It was not easy for them, but I always thank God for their understanding. I also wish to acknowledge the support of my family members: Father Emma, Bene, Glo, Chijioke, Onyema, Chika, Chumo, Kasie, Nenye, Chizuba and the entire Ugwuoke family.

I acknowledge the immense help of my mentors and friends, especially those through whom God has made me who I am today; Sir & Lady David Osunde, Sam Ikoku, Mac Attram, Dayo Olomu, Alex & Amanda Pilz, Sir Patrick Pillah etc.

I finally thank anyone who contributed towards making this work a success. I am most grateful to my editor, Mr. Malcolm Veitch, who was of utmost support. I also thank Donna Sinclair of Options4change for her great support. Finally, I thank the MD of Bifantasy Press Lagos, Mr. Chuma Igwebueze and Mr. David Okoro of Iam Bookshop, London for appreciated support and guidance. Thank and God bless you all!

WHY YOU?

Once upon a dawn
T'was your day of birth
But why were you born
To a world that yells for your help?

Your mother tried her best
To give some love and kindness
Your father did his best
But what would you offer?

These showers of love and kindness
Soon down, down dwindled
To mother smacks and father scolds
But what have you done?

A short while after
A people's cry be heard
Lamenting your sorrowful departure
But why were you born?

Chigbo Ugwuoke

FOREWORD

Time to Decide is well- timed book. It is necessary and crucial to the development of anyone who struggles with making the right career choice. On daily basis through my work and social engagement, I work with a range of young people and professionals who make do with careers that they have no passion for. They focus on bringing home enough to pay the bills and little else.

Knowing Chigbo is a real inspiration for me. He is natural at mentoring and inspiring self-worth and value. His writing is current and visionary for those of us who are yet to decide or have decided and want to explore their greatness. In my career, I am often required to lead and evidence positive outcome for services and people. There are many pages in Time to Decide that I will be using as references to inspire greatness.

Whether you have chosen the wrong career or are yet to choose, Time to Decide will boost your confidence and ability to achieve what you are already capable of. Choosing the right career for many is no easy task. Rightfully the book teaches you how to self-love, be what you love and earn the rewards for who you are. We are in an era of financial insecurities even amongst those who have jobs that pays well above the average. The need for inspiration and self-reassurance and a 'Yes I Can' attitude is influenced by mission, purpose and choice. All of these have been explored in instances in the book to strengthen our might against too many obstacles self-imposed or foreign.

In these challenging times in almost every society it is very easy to allow barriers or excuses to not let us achieve what we can as a matter of talent or course. In recent years, we have witnessed a concerning rise in poverty, absent parents, social exclusion, school exclusions, academic under achievement, social unrest and the over-representation of young people in places that have no connection with raising aspirations.

The affected seems almost incapable to set and achieve goals that lead to worthwhile career choices. When you are able to undertake rigid self-assessments of passion, dreams, personal qualities and your abilities to reflect and choose what is right for you, thereafter nothing can make you dance to anything you don't like and did not choose for yourself. Time to Decide offers us some fantastic opportunities to achieve all of these for ourselves.

The inspirations and dynamics of Time to Decide should be used to fight corners in society, make our own choices and earn the benefits of our hard work in study, skills acquirement and our determination to succeed against all odds, of culture, society pressures, politics and the opinions of your peers.

The recent increases in student fees, high competition amongst the qualified for jobs Equalities issues present platforms for debates, legislations and rationalising studying for years to obtain a qualification and a huge debt. All of these obstacles can be defeated if you sincerely keep going with your passion, uncompromised goals and dreams to become and be the best at what you do. There is no shortage of inspiration and essential tools in Time to Decide, to achieve self-love, self-belief and unrelenting determination to claim your right to be who you are making your own choices at the time that is right for you.

I recommend Time to Decide without reservation to all of us who are looking for career inspiration and purpose for ourselves or those we care about.

Congratulations Chigbo.
Donna Sinclair
Chief Executive Officer, Options 4 Change, UK

INTRODUCTION

What do you think about yourself? Are you happy with whom and where you are? Where do you want to be in the next ten years? Whoever you are, whatever you are at the moment, thank goodness, you are reading this little book at the very right time.

If most of us had read a book like this some years ago, our career stories might have been different. The good news is that it's never too late.

Close your eyes for a minute and paint a picture in your mind of where and what you want to be. What do you think will get there? What is it that you really want to do? Whatever you want to do to enable you to get where you want to be is your career.

Who is it you want to be in life? What do you want? Where do you want to be? When do you want to be there? The answers to all these questions would lead smoothly to the career of your choice.

Your career is your calling in life for which you are trained and which you intend to follow for a living. It is that calling from which you make a living. In other words, as Vincent Van Gogh says, "Your career is not what brings home your pay check. Your career is what you were put on earth to do, with such passion and such intensity that it becomes a spiritual calling."

There are as many different careers as there are needs on earth. The purpose of this book is to help you discover the career that is yours. It will help you discover a profession and a way of making a living. It will enable you to discover a career niche that brands you.

Sometimes, people think of great people and want to be like them. In every career, there are great persons worthy of emulation. Some are doctors, lawyers, drivers or painters. We can admire every successful person but we cannot aspire to be all of them. As far as career choice is concerned, you must make a choice based on who you are, not who others are. You cannot dream of being a doctor, lawyer, driver and painter at the same time. Trying to be everything and do everything would be like trying to be a jack-of-all-trades and master of none.

This boils down to choice problems. Choice is easy for some people but not for others. Career-choice mistakes can be very expensive. Some people have even gone to the extreme of committing suicide due to their career mistakes. Career is a very delicate issue, which no one can afford to leap into without careful consideration.

Life is like a market place. Some people know what they want and go straight for it. Such people are very familiar with the terrains of the life-market. They know exactly what they want and where to get it. They walk straight, pick it up, and off they go.

Some people, however, struggle in a deep ocean of career confusion. They don't know what they want to do. Their minds are muddled with their personal, parental and peer career interests. They don't know what to follow or where to follow. This book will let some fresh air into their heads and unleash the energy they need to live life abundantly in their chosen careers.

It's important to be honest with oneself while making a career choice. I remember while I was training as a Career Coach in London, I met a man who looked rather unhappy. I asked him if he was all right. When he told me his difficulties, I realised straight away that he was in the wrong class. There was yet a lady who stood up and said, "I don't think I can be a life coach because I am too judgemental." She never turned up again. The other was my friend, who told me straight away, "I think I am more bothered about my business. I won't be coming here again." And that was it.

You don't want to be the wrong key in the right padlock. You must "know thyself". The fact that your best mate wants to be a doctor should not be the reason for you to want to be a doctor. Your career is your choice and you are responsible for it.

As I said before, career-choice mistakes are very expensive and can take a long time to correct. When you choose the right career path, you enjoy your job. You become happy with everyone and everything. You look forward to Fridays because you love your family, and look forward to Mondays because you love your job. What a happy life you live when you choose your true career.

Your choice is totally yours. This book is my little helping hand to enable you to discover who you are, to choose where you want to be and when you want to get there. The book will help you discover the real you, and help you find a career you enjoy; *your* career and not someone else's.

I use the term "discover" because you are already suited to a career; you are who you are, so you just have to find what suits you. All you must do is discover your purpose in life. It's a natural extension of who you are. All I do is stand by you on this voyage of career choice.

After reading this book, you will be sure to pick a career that you enjoy and love, and are suited too, instead of despising your job and tolerating it just for the money.

Enjoy the amazing discovery of who you are and what you want to be.

TABLE OF CONTENTS

CHAPTER 1
YOU ARE WHO YOU ARE!

"To be nobody-but-yourself... in a world which is doing its best night and day, to make you everybody else... means to fight the hardest battle which any human being can fight; and never stop fighting."

- E. E. Cummings

In the graveyard, there are many great men and women who never became great. They never realized who they were until they died. For someone to live and die without discovering who they are, is a serious issue. They are better off not being born at all.

No matter how much of an accident your creation may have been, you now have a purpose, and that purpose is the essence of your life. You are a complete person but can only sense that completeness when you know who you are. You have the power to do all you can, if you believe in yourself.

Sometimes, I sit down and observe my three-year-old son, Charbel. I see in him a whole and complete person. He feels he can do anything I do. He believes he can drive. Any time he tries to take the car steering off me and I refuse, he feels let down and that makes him cry. Charbel believes he can do everything. Most people, like my son, are born whole and complete. All we need is to grow and manifest our expressions of completeness. In time, we begin to see ourselves the way others want to see us. That affects us and begins to hold us back. We begin to think we are who we are not, with many limitations. Mostly, it's not who we *are* that holds us back, it's who we think we are *not*. Our environment makes us begin to think we cannot, even when we can. Some of us conform and try to become who we are not.

Some research once involved a group of people left all alone in a conference room. None of them could open the door. They pulled the door handle and concluded they were locked in. A toddler jumped down from her mother's shoulder, and within a few minutes of fiddling, she opened the door. How did she do it? Everyone else had tried opening the door from the right-hand side and thought it was locked. When the child tried the right and it did not work, she tried the left and it worked. The child believed in herself and believed she could open the door. The door was not locked after all. The hinges were just put on the wrong side. It took a brave toddler to rectify the situation by believing she could to get everyone out of the room.

The point I am trying to make here is that you are able to do what you have to do, if you know and believe in yourself. We limit ourselves by the judgement of others. Most people consider general beliefs and expectations rather than their personal convictions. The child was able to open the door because she had not yet been conditioned by expected logical door-construction. Thus, she was naturally able to "think outside the box" because of her unconditioned self, and this led to a kind of self-belief. You yourself once had such belief until you saw people doing what you could not do. This does not mean they could do all you could. You are special and can do what you should. All you need to do is rediscover who you are and believe in yourself.

When I talk of who you are, I don't include those viral things you have learnt and experienced and that corrupted you. The real "you", without other people's expectations impressed upon it, is good enough to make you happy. Don't forget that who you are differs from what you have learnt. You need to reformat yourself and forge ahead.

If you do drugs, that is not who you are; it is what you *do* which has become a habit. No one is born a drunkard and no one is born a gangster. You are not born with drugs in your mouth. Never say, "I am a drug addict"; rather say, "I am addicted to drugs", or better still, "I abuse drugs." You must detach yourself from what you do. In that way you can work on your acts as mere habits. If you think you *are a criminal*, it's hard to change the habit, but if you think you *do criminal acts*, you can more easily stop yourself because the acts are not representative of who you are.

You are a human *being*, not a human *doing*. What you do is far from what you are. Your habits are some of that wrong stuff you have filled your life basket with. You can sort out your shopping basket by removing the unwanted stuff and filling it up with the things you desire.

Some things might have happened in your life that filled you with wrong ideas of who you are. It could be people's comments, some trials, failures or habits. Forget those. You are still who you are. Your mother could have tagged you lazy because you were not as fast as your siblings. Think! There are things you could do better and more easily than anyone else in this life. Think and be who you are, not who people think you are or who they want you to be.

I remember being second-best in my class in secondary school while failing in Maths. It did not feel good at all. I felt as if I was bad for not being able to do what others could. What I forgot was that I had a niche, something I was good at. I wanted to be who *they* were and not who I was *meant* to be. Realise who you are and appreciate what you are.

Some are ashamed of who they are. They are not confident enough to go for what they want. They are not proud to say, "I am who I am." Yet that is the only way they can be happy in life. You have to love yourself and be what you love. You cannot love yourself enough unless you become what you love to be.

Make a choice and stand for it. Michael Evans, an English soap and stage actor, reminds us that if you don't stand for something, you will fall for anything. Connect what you are doing to who you are being and you will get paid for who you are.

CHAPTER 2
YOURS IS YOURS!

When you wake up on a Monday morning, how do you feel while preparing for work? Do you spring up from the bed and zoom into the bathroom feeling happy? Some people would just turn over and go back to sleep.

In the course of one of my training events, five people were made to sleep in one room on a Sunday evening. When they woke up they were asked how they felt about the night. Four of them said they had kept waking up and wondering why the night was taking so long, whereas the other four said they had woken up at 7.00 am and felt the night had been too short and that they needed more sleep. Why was there so much difference?

Those who felt the night was too long were discovered to be happy with their careers. They looked forward to Monday and each other working day to get back to the work they loved doing. Their careers were fun. The rest were in the wrong careers. To them, Monday was a nightmare. They didn't want to go back to that same old boring job again. Their careers were the work they hated, and what made the difference were the career decisions.

The question is what do you think about yourself? Where do you want to be in the next ten years? If you are young, thank God, because you are reading this book at the very right time when you are about to make your first career decisions. If you are not so young, don't worry, because it's never too late.

So, close your eyes and imagine where and what you want to be in the next ten years. What you want to do for a living to enable you get where you want to be is your career. *Who* do you want to be? *What* do you want to be? *Where* do you want to be? The answers to these questions will determine the career you choose.

Imagine yourself waking up on a Monday morning, getting to your work place dressed the way you like, doing what you really like and getting paid for it.

You are happy at the job, and you are happy with everyone and everything. You look forward to Friday because you love your family. You look forward to Monday because you love your job. What a happy life you live!

Imagine yourself at the age of forty, waking up on a Tuesday morning with a sigh. You stand by the roadside, waiting to be hired without skills. You are out and willing to work not knowing where. You want to do anything; cleaning, plastering, painting, loading or off-loading. You can virtually do anything and everything but you are skilled in nothing. Imagine!

Imagine yourself getting up on a Wednesday morning feeling very weak, and dragging yourself up because you have to catch a train to work; then getting to the office to do what you hate most. You pray that the day ends quickly so that you can go home again. You are angry with yourself but have no option. Life must go on, the bills must be paid, and the landlord will come calling by the end of the month. What a nightmare of a life!

Imagine yourself waking up on a Thursday morning standing by the alleyway, begging for spare change. Looking up at everyone, you feel subhuman. You regret everything but you know it's your fault. Eventually you realise what you have done to yourself. There you are, a pauper, a slave to yourself, and you can't stand the sight of old friends who are more successful. What a mess of a life!

Imagine yourself waking up on a Friday morning feeling confused. You have no idea where to go, no idea what to do. You stand in misery, feeling you've lost it all.

These Monday-to-Friday illustrations create an idea of where you could be in the next ten years.

If you choose a career that is right for you, you are bound to be passionate about your job. If you choose the career that is for someone else you are bound to hate your job and be lazy and lousy at it.

To me, laziness means choosing to do what you don't want to, and being reluctant to do it. Give a "lazy man" a job he likes and you would discover he was never lazy at all. Give a hard worker the wrong job and he'll become the laziest man ever.

Any time I write on a topic I have passion for, I stay up till dawn; no coffee, no red bulls, no drugs. But when I write on a topic of no interest, I wake in the morning with my laptop in front of me and all the lights on. It's obvious that working on a topic I have a passion for is like working for fun. It's a result of passion. If you choose a career you are not interested in, then you are bound to get frustrated midway.

In the same way, you cannot achieve a career goal without love and passion for it. Even if you work hard enough you can never be fulfilled because you have not filled the gap you are born to fill. The successful person is the one who is happy in what they do.

When you close your eyes, there is first a vacuum, so search for your real self. Keep searching until you discover yourself in entirety. Discover yourself! There is a space only you can fill up, and the world needs you to fill up that space. Dale Carnegie's advice is that you throw yourself into the work of filling that space, believing in it with all your heart. *Live* for it and you will find happiness that you had thought could never be yours.

Three tourists went shopping for party dresses in the West End of London. One of them was tall and slim. The other was short and rotund, while the third was of average build. The short, rotund girl knew what was good for her but decided to try something else for a change. When the tall, slim girl tried on a light gown, the short rotund girl saw how good it was and decided to buy the same style. She took for granted the idea that since it was good for her friend, it should be good for her, too. At the party she turned up looking like an inflated parachute! No one had told her how bad she looked because she had never asked. She was a laughing stock at the dance hall and was left alone all night.

Career is like a cap; check out your head size and wear the one that fits. The advice is "know thyself". William Jennings Bryan said destiny is not a matter of chance, "It is a matter of choice: it is not to be waited for; it is a thing to be achieved".

When Adam Smith founded the principle of division of labour in his "Wealth of Nations", he did not really know how well it would fit into career lives. Every being has a role to play in life. Every man is born for a purpose. You are equipped with all you need. You have the skills already, so all you have to do is develop them, and become a *round* peg in a round hole. Your life is made to fit the purpose of your existence. If you discover who you are and your purpose, life becomes easy and fun.

I remember an expensive career-choice blunder I committed when I finished junior secondary exams and had to choose subjects for my senior class. Though I did well in arts subjects and social sciences, I wanted to study science because I thought it was in vogue. I knew I was no good at Mathematics, Chemistry and Physics, but I chose them due to other people's interests.

I started missing classes because I wasn't happy any more. It was a terrible experience. I became miserable trying to learn Physics, Chemistry and Maths, having dropped Fine and Applied Arts and English literature, which were my best subjects.

I wasted my first year in senior class struggling to learn things I did not enjoy. After that year, I had to drop physics because it made no sense to me. It was too late for me to go back to my passions of Literature and Arts. The ghost of this mistake followed me until I reached university. I had to go back to secondary school to study literature because I couldn't study law without it. It cost me a lot of time and money before I could amend this blunder.

Some people are not happy with who they are and what they do. They are stuck with a job they hate with a passion. For such people there is no remedy unless they seek help, and they must change before it's too late. Such people unleash aggression on their family and friends without knowing why. They are just not happy. Imagine how many families have broken up due to one of the partners not being happy with his or her career. You have to do what you love to do. Be yourself.

Listen to what the great artist Pablo Picasso had to say: "My mother said to me, 'If you become a soldier, you'll be a general, if you become a monk you'll end up as the pope.' Instead, I became a painter and wound up as Picasso." Isn't that amazing? Pablo followed his painting passion and ended up being himself, a great painter of his time.

I once read in the dailies of a big-time "successful" lawyer who committed suicide. I asked myself, how successful could this lawyer have been? To people who knew him, he seemed successful but he personally knew he was a failure. He hated himself and his job to such an extent that he jumped from a skyscraper. Why? He had chosen the wrong career and was merely a successful slave to it. In his suicide note he said he didn't have a life. One can succeed as a slave, but cannot be happy as a slave. That was the issue.

According to Harland Sanders you have to like your work. You have to like what you are doing. You have got to be doing something worthwhile so you can like it - because it's worthwhile. Everyone in this world is created for a reason. There is a gap for you to fill. The question is "what is that gap?" Most people stand in the way of their own career by trying to do what others want them to do. The fact is that there is an assignment for everyone on earth. Something only you can do the way it's meant to be done. This assignment is what makes everyone different, and that is what a good career means.

Accept who you are and the way you are. Be happy because you are special. Whatever you are, there is something you have that you can get paid for. Make no mistake about that.

Ibert Hubbard says "every man's work, whether it be literature or music or pictures or architecture or anything else, is always a portrait of himself." Don't be afraid to choose a career that might be unacceptable to your family and friends. Different people have different duties assigned to them by nature. Nature has given you the power or the desire to do what only you can. Each dog must bark with his own throat.

If you think about it, there must be something you ought to have done which you feel is still undone. What is it you feel you should have accomplished that you have not? Think, you have a mission and that is your life's purpose. Choose it!

When your career is your choice, you become more challenged to succeed in it. *Know what you want and go for it.*

Make no more mistakes.

CHAPTER 3
WHOSE MUSIC ARE YOU DANCING TO?

Those who know me well know that I love dancing a lot. When I go to parties, I consider the sole purpose of music is to be danced to. I dance a lot, but sometimes the DJ gets caught up in a certain kind of music I disliked. So I usually leave the dance floor and wait for my favorite tune to play again. Sometimes I kindly request the DJ to play some favorite song of mine, or a special kind of music to dance to, and off I go again.

Okay, what has that got to do with you and your career? The answer is: more than you could know. The first day I went clubbing in England, there was some music I did not really enjoy but I didn't quit, I just went on jumping instead. The tracks were hot, fast and over-spiced for my taste.

Everyone was sweating it out but I couldn't cope. Cool rhyme and rhythm were my idea of music, but this music seemed more like gymnastics to me, yet everyone loved it, so I jumped on.

When I took my English friends to an African party, I noticed that afro tunes didn't make much sense to them either. However, once we were all a bit tipsy, everyone jumped into the stage and managed to dance. My people bent down to do their style while my friends danced out of rhythm. That was the best they could do for all they cared. I also remember some times when my dad had to come into my room to turn off my sound system. To him the music was noise but to me it was my favourite Snoop.

You see the point? Everyone has his or her own kind of music. Each time I sit down because I don't like a song, I realize it is actually a favourite of someone, somewhere. I realize that one man's meat is another's poison. If you realize who you are, you must realize what you want, too.

Any time I dance to a tune I don't like, I am dancing to another person's music, so I inevitably ask myself at all times, "Whose music am I dancing to?"

There are so many of us who are dancing to other people's music. You try to move and sway to the rhythm, but it doesn't fit in the heart. You just go through the motions. Everybody else seems to be happily dancing, but you just cannot manage to tune in. Think… It's not your music!

We all have unique life songs in our hearts; songs assigned by nature and specially designed for us to dance to. Your song is designed to keep you on the dance floor forever if only you can listen to it properly. You'll never tire of it because it's so deeply rooted in your innermost being. It's your passion, your dream. Whether we choose to listen to our music or not, it always pulls at our hearts, calling us to the dance floor.

So, I want to ask you: whose music are you dancing to? What can you offer the world that no one else can?

CHAPTER 4
YOUR LIFE IS FOR A PURPOSE!

Listen to yourself and your heart. Great people dream and make their career out of what they love. Singing songs, cooking meals, working with numbers, networking with people and writing essays are all valuable talents. What do you usually enjoy doing, without being asked? What do you seem to be naturally good at? On what do you focus best or most enthusiastically? What must you be dragged away from doing? What do you usually do when you have free time? By listening to what you truly enjoy doing; you can shape your career path.

Here are nine questions to help you discover your unique purpose in life:

In what area do others ask you for help?
This is an area where our distinct talents scream at us. Close relatives and friends will readily pinpoint our strengths that we offer them when they need assistance of a certain kind.

What did you love doing as a child?
Most of us had our favourite activities as kids, but often they were not furthered, because they were not deemed important enough. Time and time again, traditional education methods displace our passion.

Retrace your steps. Look back at what you enjoyed as a child, and remember your interests, hobbies and activities. Usually we are asked about what we want to be at an early age. Try to remember what you wrote down or said to your teacher, family or friends. What did you say you wanted to be when you grew up?

What are you good at?
What do you do well? What are your natural interests and inclinations? Music, sports, food, mechanics, communication, talking, acting, or caring? What gives you a sense of achievement? Although this question is obvious, many of us have a hard time identifying our strengths, because they are often associated with something we do every day, and it's just not spectacular enough.

David Beckham makes waves in soccer because he is good at it. He chose to become a footballer because he discovered he had what it took. He did not choose to be a footballer just to make money. He enjoyed it and still enjoys it, and so he does it well and gets paid for it.

Richard Branson, the British business mogul, says, "a business has to be involving, it has to be fun, and it has to exercise your creative instincts."

What makes you unique?
You know the best qualities that make you unique; you know the special natural gifts you have. These are the things that can enable you to discover your purpose in life and choose the career that is right for you. That is where you will succeed. Abraham Maslow once said that "a musician must make his music, a painter must paint, a poet must write if he is to ultimately be at peace with himself."

What are you not good at?
What can you not do well? Orion Swett Marden says, "One necessary ingredient of a career is the necessity to analyze what you haven't got as well as what you have got." Having discovered what you are good at and embraced it, you must also discover what you are not good at and deemphasize it. Having answered the question "what can I do?" you must also be able to answer the question, "what can I *not* do?"

Consider any natural conditions that may come between you and your career. This is important because if it is not considered, you may make a grievous mistake that could cause you a lifetime of misery.

While I was a student in London, Felix, a friend of mine was a *slinger*. He earned fifteen pound per hour and worked nine hours a night. At that time I was earning far less than that working on the escalators all night after studying all day. To increase my income, I decided to become a *slinger* too. The *slinger* training cost me over a thousand pounds.

When I got my first job as a *slinger*, I resigned after two days. Why? The job involved climbing up and down very high scaffoldings. Felix never knew I feared heights, but I had to climb as high as the tenth floor of an unfinished building through the scaffolds, and I felt I was going to be blown off by the winds each time I lifted a leg.

I couldn't do that job for all the money in the Bank of England. It was either the job was not right for me or I was not the right man for the job. You must ask yourself: what always seems to be a struggle? What makes you feel awkward or out of place? For instance, some people are great talkers but hate writing; for others, it's the other way around. That's not to say you can't develop skills and strategies in areas that are not your forte, but if you choose to do so, you will always know that they are not actually your main strengths.

What do you want to dream of when your head hits the pillow at night?

If you were to design your dream-job, what would it be like? Where would you be and what would you be doing in that job? Your dream is important. Together with your gifts and talents, there is a dream in your heart, because that's what drives us on through life. Now, that dream, as unachievable as it may seem, will constantly be pulling at your heart. Identify your true values, because they are very important in choosing your career. They determine your courses of action or outcomes and reflect your sense of right and wrong. If you believe equal rights are for all, don't choose a career that is not egalitarian. You will surely be frustrated and unproductive. If you believe people should not be killed for any reason during wars, don't join the army. Your attitude and behaviour will be more positive if your career aligns with your beliefs.

What lifestyle do you want to live? What are your beliefs? What religion or ethical guidelines do you follow? What type of organization or people do you want to work for? What product or service do you want to contribute towards?

If you were ever to write a book, what would it be about?

Even if you are not a writer, just ask yourself what your favourite topic is likely to be. You will always pick something you are confident to share information about, because you are good at it.

What is the activity you most enjoy during your day?

Even though it might be totally insignificant to you, like cooking or sewing, or training your dog, it will help you pinpoint what you are really passionate about. What sort of things do you like to read about, or talk about? What shows do you watch on television? What magazine and newspaper articles catch your eye?

What do people tell you about yourself?

Do they notice that you light up when you explain something? Does everybody seem to compliment you on your writing, your story-telling skills, or physical co-ordination?

B. A. Billings once said that every individual is special. "If I had one gift that I could give you, my friend, it would be the ability to see yourself as others see you, because only then would you know how extremely special you are." You are born with special, natural potential. The qualities that make you special are different from skills, in that they tend to be innate rather than learned. Once found, they can be nurtured and developed, but finding them can be tricky. It's partly a process of self-observation and honesty. Discover what works and what doesn't work you.

The world is a market place; be there for the right reason. Don't fill your shopping basket with the wrong stuff - the untradable skills and certificates that earn you nothing. You can be learned but still not successful. Discover the best of you and go for it!

CHAPTER 5
DO THE POSSIBLE

A journey of two thousand miles begins with one step. Once you have identified your talents and gifts, ask yourself what can be done to further them. How would you do that? What resources are at your disposal now? When you have made up your mind what to do, think of the next step. Everything done in this life starts with a first step, so don't just fold your arms and hope for miracles. You must do something for something to happen. The miracle worker is seated calmly in the corner waiting for you to do the *possible*.

The short man Zacheus wanted to see Jesus (Isa) but was too short to look over other people's shoulders. He did something about it that changed his life. He ran ahead of the crowd and climbed a tree. Because of his effort, Jesus followed him to his house and dined with him. We might be as short as Zacheus in our career. We may not know where to start but we have to start somewhere. Keep moving and get out of your own way. Zacheus was too short but there was *something* he could do. Run ahead and climb the tree of your career now. Get out of your own way.

Robert Tilton says that while we wait for God to do the impossible, he is waiting for us to do the possible. Now, whether you believe in God or not, the point is that nothing comes of nothing, whereas action leads to more action through its knock-on effect. When I thought of becoming a life coach, I did the first thing I could. I went to Google. There, on the first page, I saw an advert offering free training for coaching. That was amazing! I booked for that preliminary training immediately and never looked back. More doors opened continually after that.

In the words of Thomas Carlyle, "Blessed is he who has found his work; let him ask no other blessedness."

According to Brian Tracy, success reveals itself one step at a time. Your career might seem very scary and impossible, but don't worry. Take the first step with faith. You need to believe in what you want. If you desire it passionately, just move on with faith, and one step will lead to another. Don't start with what you cannot do, but with what you can.

Remember the story of David (Daud) and Goliath (Jalut) in Israel. Israel is one of the rockiest places on earth. The Israelites trod daily on the millions of stones and never knew their significance. David was able to save the whole nation with just one of those stones. He discovered the significance of the insignificant. David did what was possible when he hurled a stone at the forehead of the giant Philistine. The impossible happened instantly: the stone penetrated Goliath's (Jalut's) forehead and he died.

Everything great starts with something small. The painting on the ceiling of the Sistine chapel would have been impossible if Michelangelo had not done what was possible. Lying on his back, the great artist painted the nine Old Testament stories on the eighty-five-foot-high ceiling. This great artwork started with one brush stroke. It must have taken courage to start but it took four and half years for Michelangelo to accomplish this great work. That is the work that has made him so famous. When responding to an interviewer he said, "If people knew how hard I worked to get my mastery, it wouldn't seem so wonderful after all."

Whatever your goal is, you can do it. All you need is to do the possible. You have the brush in your hands; start with one brush stroke at a time. You have the stone in your sling, so strike before Goliath does. One word at a time you started reading this book, and soon it will be over and you'll have all the inspiration you need.

CHAPTER 6
CHOOSE FRIENDS CAREFULLY!

(It's better to be alone than to keep bad friends!)

"Keep away from people who try to belittle your ambitions. Small people always do that, but the really great people make you feel that you too can become great."
- Mark Twain

On your career voyage, you must be careful who accompanies you. Whatever career direction you choose in life, there are always people who have gone the same way, so find them! Also, there are always people who want to go the same way; find them and go with them. The old adage says two minds are better than one.

I remember my first day ever in school. I can still hear the voice of my late mother, who told me to find out who was the most intelligent person in my class and make him a friend. I did and it helped me greatly. I always felt challenged by people who did better than I, and it made me work harder. From then on I have always been in the company of the best, wherever I find myself. It makes me set high standards for myself at all times.

Go with fools and you end up a fool. If you go with wise people, definitely you shall be wise. That's why they say, "Show me who you go with and I will tell you who you are." A bad friend is like a virus that corrupts your system. Their talk distorts your wisdom and upsets your plans. They make you lose focus and forget your goals. Bad friends want you to be the same as them.

Surround yourself with a wise circle of friends. They are the only known antivirus hardware that can protect you against bad companions. Do not give the wrong people the chance to seduce you with their destructive habits.

Discover your goals and believe in them. Any person who does not believe in your goals should not be listened to. Be sure about your career goal and believe in yourself. The good book says, "Do not be yoked together with unbelievers; for what fellowship hath righteousness..." The book of proverbs also says that a violent man enticeth his neighbour, and leadeth him into the way that is not good" (Proverbs 16:29).

Make your goals very clear and believe in them. If any of your friends don't believe in your goals, get ready to say goodbye. If any of them don't want what you want, that might be the virus you need to debug. Waste no time. Wrong friends should not be given a chance in your life. If you are blind, don't be led by the blind man. Seek out your real friends.

As St. Paul said, "Be not deceived, evil communications corrupt good manners" (1 corinthians 15:33). Remember also that good communication corrects bad manners. Good communication is as stimulating as a black coffee and just as hard to sleep after (Anne Morrow Lindbergh).

Discover where successful people are and go with them. Join clubs and organisations in line with who you want to be. When I was at university, I joined the Rotaract Club, and I found the right friends there. They all became successful people, and they were always ready to lift me up. Look for the right friends; find them wherever they may be. If you wanted to be a gangster, you'd know where to find your mates. If you wanted to be a robber, you'd know where to find your mates. If you were a yes man you'd need to join the 'yes' group. Since I joined the Knights of St. Columba in London, I've had a body of mentors who support me at every minute. It's easy for them to lift me up because they are up already.

Watch out for bad friends and avoid them. Always look before you leap. Monitor people's behaviour before you start hanging out with them. If you meet two people that don't fit into your life goals, introduce them to each other and keep moving. Eventually they'll see they have no place in your life and leave you alone. Seek out your true friends.

CHAPTER 7
TAKE A LEAP OUT OF YOUR COMFORT ZONE

I had this funny thing happen to me once. Well, at least it's funny now. I wanted to share it with you so you know that you are not alone in going through your issues, and that we are all living through times of trials and tribulations. Resolutions are about stepping out of your comfort zone and moving your life forward to get what you want.

Everyone goes through moments of not wanting to do certain things; things that make them uneasy or uncomfortable. It's human nature to want to stay where we feel secure, where we know what's happening. We don't always want to learn something new. It's the easy way out; it's comfortable. Why shake a healthy tooth?

The story I am about to tell you turned out to be quite an "aha!" moment for me. You see, it started out with me thinking that it would be fun to do something different. Before I qualified to practise law in England and Wales, I worked as a lift and escalator man for the London Underground. I worked in the night and studied during the day. Because of the relatively good pay and the nature of the job, it was a good example of a comfort zone. I sat by the escalators, ensuring that movement was safe at all times. I would sit down and read newspapers and anything I could lay my hands on till dawn. I would go home and sleep till my wife woke me up for lunch. The job was easy, night after night, and paid very well.

Though I was well paid, I was losing my confidence as a lawyer. I felt I was wasting my life with the routine of looking after lifts and escalators all night. Even so, I did not want to step out of this very comfortable zone. I thought it wasn't really possible for me to practise law in the UK because I had been warned how difficult it was to pass the professional exam and how unaffordable it was, anyway. I kept procrastinating due to fear of leaving the comfort zone.

One day I arrived at work and was told that it was over. My manager said, "I'm afraid Balfour Beatty doesn't need a lift and escalator man anymore." I got seven days' notice. Then it dawned on me how important that job was to my family. My wife, our son and I were left with no source of income.

My wife encouraged me as usual, and I had no option but to step out of my comfort zone. I took a job in a construction site that paid fifty percent less than the Underground did, and it was hard manual work, harder than I had ever imagined. The pay was simply unacceptable and not enough for my family and me.

At that point I remembered I was a lawyer! It was time to decide. I had to make the first move. Zing! I was on the Law Society website. Bang! I was reading for the exams. Phew! I was enrolled to practice law in the UK eight months later. As soon as I made that shift from the comfort zone, the rest of the doors started opening.

The most important thing about this whole story is that it shows you don't have to be sure of everything on the path ahead; just be sure of the next step. Don't wait till all the lights are green because that's not going to happen. You must make a decision to move forward. The initial leap must be made with faith.

Just try to give it your best shot, no matter what it is. Getting out of your comfort zone is the most important thing. It wasn't quite as easy as it sounds, but the bridge to the comfort zone had been burnt and there was simply no going back.

My question to you is: what is holding you back from getting what you want? Now is the time to decide and to act. If you don't move your life forward, who will? You have a choice: to move forward now or to stay where you are and be forever frustrated by not having followed your dream. The decision is yours to make.

Remember, giving up is not an option. To get out of your comfort zone, you must watch out for the cankerworms that nip your ideas in the bud.

The first step is to explore your options of getting paid for what you can and like to do. Search the Internet for careers that exist. Some people are unaware of certain professions and tend to feel stuck in one place without options. Talk to a career advisor. Take a career test and see what you are best suited for. See if it is something you would like to do in life. You can even do an internship to experience a particular type of career and see how it fits. If you enjoy what you do, is it really work?

Again, the Internet has opened up job opportunities in unlikely places. The fast pace of the cyber world indicates that if something doesn't exist today, check back soon because it's likely to be there tomorrow. You can either find someone willing to pay for your talents, or you can create your own opportunities.

The second step is to overcome your fear of what people will think of you. Think about the most successful people you've come across in your life. Odds are, they made some mistakes but weren't afraid of doing so. They learned from those mistakes and ploughed on. Listen to your coach who is committed to your commitment and not the journalist who is committed to his story. You're allowed to be less than perfect, and you may find that people like you more for it, because it makes you a more exciting person to be around. People are bound to applaud you when you succeed.

Thirdly, beware of Mr. Chicken Little who, according to the story, went around announcing that the sky was falling down. There are hundreds of subtle fears we bow to every day, yet the chances of their happening are so slim. It's good to be proactive, but it's bad to let a significant portion of your life be devoted to averting things that never happen… little things that could turn into adventures or funny stories if you allow yourself to deal with a little discomfort.

The fourth factor is that you have to be ready to take risks. Your comfort zone is comfortable because it is where you know what to expect. Going out on a limb can be scary because you might fail. You might lose something. But you might also gain something... In order to become comfortable with that uncertainty, you'll need to practice the following:

Be detached from your risks
When you decide to do something, do it for its own sake, not so that you can get a particular result. If you gamble, gamble with money you're ready and willing to lose; gamble for the fun and exhilaration of gambling. If you win, that's icing on the cake! If you lose, it's no big deal. In other words, let go of your attachment to a certain outcome.

Instead, focus on the joy of doing whatever you're doing. Live in the moment.

Accept every outcome in good faith

When things don't go your way, and they won't always, shrug them off. If you're clinging to your comfort zone, you're hanging on to the notion that the world is supposed to be a safe, predictable place, and that's an illusion. You're setting yourself up for frustration and disappointment. Open your eyes. The world is a dynamic place where things go right *and* wrong. That's just the way it is! Be brave.

Fifthly, you must watch out for Treasure Guards. Meat has bones and roses have thorns. Nothing good comes easily. There is a price to pay for everything. In every hero's journey, there is a treasure guard and a battle to be won. Your career is a treasure and you must be ready to fight the treasure guards. Either you win or you lose. There is no kingdom without a cross.

You must adopt the principle of "no retreat, no surrender" to win. Don't forget, to win you must not quit. You must stand by your career goals. For better and for worse, it is you and your career. You simply decide not to quit, and that's that. Your treasure is yours.

CHAPTER 8
WORK LIKE A BEE!

"He who does not work let him not eat."

He who asks God for rain must prepare his field. The man who has had sufficient sleep has no reason for not getting off the bed when he wakes. Time is a precious tool for every career. Time must be used and not wasted. A sleeping cat catches no mouse. The warrior who drops his armour never beats the enemy.

There are four known ways one can make money; steal, borrow, beg or work. Money is never plucked from a tree. There is no meat without bone and there is no honey without bees. Among all the ways of making money, the noblest way is to work for it. For any career to be successful there has to be hard work. As Dale Carnegie would always say, "there is no substitute for hard work."

Like it or not, you are here for a higher purpose than merely eating, drinking and sleeping, because ambition is what ultimately drives us on to experience the extraordinary human gifts of intellectual prowess and laughter. Make the most of your human extraordinariness. Find your niche. Work it out.

The wonderful thing is that our purpose is way beyond our wildest dreams. It is vastly bigger than we can imagine, and way above our capacity to comprehend, yet incredibly exciting to follow. That is exactly why many choose *not* to follow it! Although we have the dreams in our hearts, many of us just can't believe they can ever come true. Yet dream plus work equals reality. Wake up to work and realize the innate dreams that yearn in your heart.

Ensure you don't indulge in time-killing activities. Success comes only when you manage your time effectively. Real success comes when you fill your time with meaningful and fruitful tasks. This is the time for you to act.

I remember my mate at university who was a great time-killer. All his mates went years ahead of him in school. He still hasn't been able to catch up. He graduated with a poor grade, three years after all his mates. Think of all the time killers in your life and check them out ten years from now. They'll be unskilled, confused, lacking focus, and mired in regret.

This is the time for you to ask yourself the question, "What can I do with my time?" The answer is to discover your career and work towards it. This would make a lot of difference between you and your mates. Waste no further time with those without a future. Find your mates and work along with them.

Spend your time wisely. Make a timetable and a daily to-do list and work hard to follow it. Have a set purpose and a daily target. Don't leave till tomorrow what you can do today. Avoid procrastination, the greatest stealer of time and the lazy man's excuse.

The best time to succeed is now. He who cannot when he may, may find he may not when he can. Use your time well and reap the rewards you seek. Time wasted is regret begun. The bee that makes the sweetest honey never stays in the hive.

The essence of our career is that we can earn a living through it. The yardstick of measuring our success is how comfortably we can meet our basic needs. It all boils down to money. Career Success without money is like a house without a roof.

Hamilton Holt says that nothing worthwhile comes easily. "Work, continuous work and hard work, is the only way to accomplish results that last." Nothing good comes for nothing.

On my way to work one early morning, I watched bees hovering and buzzing over some roses in our neighbour's garden. I stood and observed them for a while.

Without a break, they searched for nectar from flower to flower. On my way back from work, I saw the bees still working as hard as before. It is wonderful how hard these bees work. At the end of the hassle, the result of their labour is the honey. Honey for the whole world. Indira Gandhi was right when he said that there are two kinds of people, those who do the work and those who take the credit. We all take honey but ignore its cost to the bees that make it. Gandhi's advice is

"Try to be in the first group; there is less competition there." So it boils down to the issue of work as the only option.

A will to work is the most priceless virtue. Work is the only natural opportunity for anyone to design their future. You must be willing to work to achieve your career goal. Sit up and remove all the distractions and obstacles. Get out of your own way. You are the greatest obstacle to your own career success. Work and work for gain. He who does not work for gain may never gain from his work. The amount of calories burnt is not a good measure for work done. Hard work is more to do with results. What is your aim?

What problems will you solve with your career and get paid for doing so? Work today to be free tomorrow. Learn from the bees. Nectar is sweet but the bees save it to make honey. Sacrifice today for future gains. The bees could consume the nectar and forget the honey, but they do not. They are focused on their goal... to make honey. Do not waste your time and energy. Be focused on your career goal. Discover your dreams and wake up to the challenges of realising them. The bee guards jealously what it has worked for. The bees say that he who does not work shall not eat. That is why they sting anyone who tries to steal the honey they have laboured so hard for.

Great people not only dream dreams but wake up to the challenges they bring. Martin Luther King had a dream and died for it to come true. Lay the foundation stones of your career on hard work today and stand out tomorrow. Mandela paid his dues in the prison, Martin Luther King had to die. What would you sacrifice?

Hard work is not too much a price for you to pay. Be committed to your career goal!

CHAPTER 9
DESIRE TO BE GREAT!

Whether you are the man standing by the roadside waiting to be hired without skills, or you are flipping hamburgers at some unknown fast food store in the middle of nowhere, or you're about to receive a Cambridge degree, you were fashioned for greatness.

Yes, in each one of us I believe there is somebody great who is destined to be a blessing, to impact other lives, to change the world, and to give an important legacy to this planet.

Now that you have embarked on the discovery of your purpose, greatness is not beyond your reach anymore. You have been marked for success and you are empowered to prosper and succeed.

Do these thoughts awaken a picture of your future in your heart? Does this conversation spark up a plan? Are you feeling challenged to step out and set higher goals for yourself? I answer yes on your behalf because I trust you can do it.

There are no limits to what you can do with your career if it is truly yours. All you need do is set a goal, make a plan, and desire. He who does not know who he is looking for will not know when he meets him. Be clear in your mind what you want. Set goals and plan. Our limitations are self-imposed, and they only exist in our minds.

Whatever thoughts you are feeding your mind with today will determine where you are going to be tomorrow.

My Irish friend bought his son a turtle for his birthday about five years ago. The turtle came in a little aquarium and was really tiny and cute back then. As time went by the turtle started to grow, and soon my friend had to purchase a bigger aquarium. Of course, the turtle kept on growing. She outgrew three aquariums and my friend was getting worried. Pictures of giant turtles crawling around his house were starting to haunt his mind.

He was concerned and sought help from a friend who had six turtles. He was advised not to change the aquarium any more. He was made to realize that these turtles could really get huge, but, if you limited their living space, they would stop growing.

Now that's interesting! It made me think about how the world is crowded with creatures that are limited by their surroundings and the influences they expose themselves to.

They are called human beings. And the vast majority of them live at a much lower level than they were created for. What is holding them back? What is limiting their growth? Basically, it is the information they are feeding their minds on.

Our brains are filled up with negative messages such as "I cannot", "I am lazy", "I am rough", "I am inferior", "if only I were still single", "I am unlucky", "If only my father were rich", "I can never achieve anything", and so on.

Whatever the case, these negative feelings are not true about you. Whom are you listening to? What is your purpose? What is your desire? What is your goal? Whatever your goal is, heaven is your limit.

Fill yourself with positive desires. Want it and you have it. Surround yourself with positive people and you will be infected with positive desires. Are you poor and shallow in mind? It is easy to tell what is in your mind by listening to what comes out of your mouth. "Out of the abundance of the heart the mouth speaks." What are the people that surround you daily telling you? Are they always talking about how bad things are, or how difficult life is? Who is your mentor? Is he or she an inspiring role model? What does your teacher say? Does she call you a ne'er-do-well? What voices are you exposing yourself to: the media, the bad news, the journalists and frivolities of life? What does the preacher of your mind call you? A wretched sinner saved by grace or a miserable sinner doomed for hell? This is the time to decide!

Let us be honest with ourselves, and assess where we are. Find out where we have missed out, and make the necessary changes to develop our innate talents. Let us de-clutter our life of unnecessary things, and seek the wisdom to peel away all the damaging influences that have invaded our lives.

Get out of the aquarium and go find yourself a big pond. Make that pond a lake. Shift your life into a higher gear now.

Refuse to be limited. It should be impossible for anybody to convince you that you are not blessed. Your whole life force is with you, and that is the best success formula that has ever existed.

A low-income shop cashier once desired to be great. He did not know what to do, but he knew what he wanted. He studied law by self-effort before he discovered his career in politics. The man was Abraham Lincoln, a past American president. He was always driven not by inherited wealth but by his desire to be great in his career.

Nelson Mandela too had that feeling of importance and desire to be great. His feeling of importance sustained him for twenty-one years in prison. He desired to be great and was great.

Nnamdi Azikiwe (Zik of Africa) left his civil service job in Nigeria at the age of 21 and travelled to America for further studies. In America, he was poverty-stricken and depressed. He once considered suicide but was sustained by his feeling of importance and the desire to be great. He later became the first president of Nigeria and one of the greatest Black Africans that ever lived.

Alezander Amosu, a Nigerian who referred to himself as "the African boy in the corner of the lunch hall that no one ever noticed" made his first million pounds at the age of twenty-two. He said he was challenged by the desire to be popular. He desired to be great and became great. He said, "The fact that I don't want to be poor is what drives me to keep coming up with brilliant ideas."

Among those who desire to be great live those who are not bothered at all. They just want to exist, and are happy to do just that. They are not motivated because they have no desire to move beyond where they are. They end up not planning their lives. At a later age they become a problem to society as skivers, gamblers, thieves, drunks and addicts of all sorts.

When I was called to the Nigerian bar in 2000, five blind people were among those called to bar as well; one of them was a young girl. These people would have been street beggars and nuisances to society if they had not acted on the desire to be great. All these blind people needed to do was decide, "I want to be a lawyer" and everything else followed.

When you have chosen your career in line with your nature, it is the time to nurture it with a desire for success. To desire is to wish for or want something. Yes, you are who you are, your career is what it is, but one thing remains. You have been given the right to choose. What to be or not to be? What do you desire?

Professor John Dervey, one of America's greatest philosophers, says that among all the desires of man, the most urging is the desire to be great. Dale Carnegie describes it a bit differently. He calls it the feeling of importance. What you desire is what you get. The desire to be great is what makes the difference between men. Desire creates motivation. When you desire it you reach out for it.

What do you want in your life? How do you feel about yourself? It matters so much how you feel about yourself. If you don't see yourself as an important being then there is a problem. Do you love who you are? If you don't, then there is a problem. When you discover who you are, you will definitely love yourself and desire to make things work. Don't punish yourself by being who you are not. Discover yourself and desire to be who you have to be. According to Bobby Unser, desire is the one secret of every man's career success. "Not education. Not being born with hidden talents. Desire!"

Another great man of our time is Sir Richard Nicholas Branson. He is the son of a barrister and the grandson of a judge born in London. He was educated at Scaitcliffe School until the age of thirteen. He then attended Stowe School until he was sixteen.

At school, young Branson was diagnosed as having dyslexia. He lacked interest in letters and words and also had problems with reading and spelling. He always put letters and figures the wrong way round and was slow at written work. He generally lacked concentration. As a result, he had poor academic performance as a student, but moved on with life, nevertheless.

Propelled by the desire to be great, he discovered his career in business. Instead of regretting and moaning over his learning problems, he moved on and established his first successful business venture at the age of 16, when he published a magazine called 'Student'. Today, Richard Branson is one of Britain's greatest industrialists, best known for his Virgin brand of over 360 companies. According to Forbes' 2009 list of billionaires, he was the 261st richest person in the world with an estimated net worth of approximately 2.6 billion pounds. Wonderful, isn't it?

The desire to be great makes a man alive and makes him work hard enough to sustain his hopes. No one gets anywhere without the desire to be there. Without the sense of importance you can never be important. Without a desire to be great you will never be great. You must want it to get it. Against all odds, Richard Branson desired to be great and became great at a very early age. The book of Proverbs says "for as a man thinks in his heart, so is he."

CHAPTER 10
DECISION TIME

How do you set your career goal?
Having made up your mind who you want to be in life, what you want do, where you want to be and when you want to be there, the next step is to put them together into a goal.

What is a goal?
You must have heard the term goal used in hockey, soccer and football. You've heard it used in space programs, fund raising, politics and peace-keeping missions. But what does a "goal" really mean in your own life?

Most dictionaries define the term "goal" as a point marking an end; the object of effort or ambition; a destination. I want to add to that for our context, and define it as: "A specific measureable state, object or accomplishment that I would like to achieve or obtain in the future, and for which I develop concrete action plans to take me there."

The significance of this definition is that it not only points to a place where you want to end up, but reminds you of the need for action to get there. A goal statement is an investment in yourself; it clearly identifies what YOU want, how you will get it, and when you will get it.

What is a career goal?
A career goal, therefore, is a goal that you set for your career path. It can be anything from your career choice to where you want to be in your career in a certain number of years. A career defines how you want to spend a large part of your life, so career-goal setting is something that everyone should do regardless of what career they choose. If you don't already have a career that you want, please read my book, *Time to Decide*.

What is your vision of career success? The image is different for each of us. For one person it's having the corner office, for another it's having a flexible schedule with plenty of time off to be with their kids.

But, whatever your dream, setting SMART goals will help you make it come true.

What is a smart career goal?

SMART is an acronym that career experts use to explain what good career goals should consist of. It means **S**pecific, **M**easurable, **A**chievable, **R**ealistic and **T**ime-framed.

A SMART career goal, therefore, is more than a vague statement like, "I will find a new job soon" or "I will become successful in two years' time." It means creating a written plan that includes reasonable and measurable long-term and short-term objectives.

Specific: Career goals need to be specific. A football field with no specific goal post is a mere playground. He who is not sure of where the goal is can never score.

Often we set career goals that are so loose it's nearly impossible to judge when we hit them or not. For example, a statement like "I will be a professional" is too vague. How will you know where to start? How do you know if and when you've reached the goal? Saying, "I will be an orthopaedic surgeon by the year 2020" is more specific. At the end of the year 2020, it will be a simple matter of whether I have become an orthopaedic surgeon or not.

Measurable: Career goals need to be measurable. For example, many of us want to increase our number of clients, but the phrase "getting new clients" simply avoids the question of "how". A clearer objective is "I will attend four networking events each month and try to get one client at each." It's a simple, concrete goal. This makes it easy to see if you hit your target or not.

Achievable: Goals need to be reasonable and achievable. Nearly everyone has tried to increase their income at one time or another. Often their success or failure depends on setting practical goals. Making a million pounds profit in 30 days as a beginner is rarely achievable. Making five to ten thousand in 30 days as a beginner is highly achievable, depending on what you do. Don't set yourself up for failure by setting goals that are out of reach.

Realistic: Goals need to be realistic. When we were kids we thought we could do anything. As adults we learn that while we can have much, we can't have it all at the same time. It's important to honestly evaluate yourself. Do you have the ability and commitment to make your dream come true? Or does it need a little adjustment? For example, you may want to be a singer, but do you have the voice, time, talent and commitment, or the X factor it takes to become a pro? To be realistic, you must be honest with yourself.

Time-framed: Goals need to have a time frame. Having a set amount of time will give your goals structure. For example, you may want to find a new job or start your own business. Why not time yourself? It is better to say, I will start a new business by 2013. Many people spend a lot of time talking about what they would like to do someday, but without an end date there is no sense of urgency, no reason to take any action today. Having a specific time frame gives you the impetus to get started. It also helps you monitor your progress.

Setting goals is more than deciding what you want to do. It involves figuring out what you need to do to get where you want to go and how long it will take you to get there.

Now you know the fundamentals of goal setting. Keep the **SMART** acronym in mind to help you remember the basics. The next step is translating this process to fit your needs.

Get started today by determining what you want. Once you know what you want you're ready to create your goals. Start with your long-term objectives. These are things you want to accomplish by the end of the year. Next, establish short-term goals. These include monthly, weekly and even daily targets that will move you toward your long-term objectives.

Be careful not to push yourself too hard or too fast. While successful people know they have to stretch their talents to grow, they also know it's important to set reasonable goals. Always be your own best friend. Never set yourself up for failure.

The first step to success is knowing where you want to go. The second step is having a plan to get there. Your goals are your road map. Follow them and you'll be well on your way.

CHAPTER 11
SALIENT QUESTIONS FOR YOU

These questions may help you decide on the exact nature
of your career choice.

1. Should you start a business or buy one?
Statistics show that something like nine out of every ten new
businesses fail within the first two years. Not all the people who own
these businesses lose money - a lot of them just decide that running
their own business is not for them or they do not obtain enough
business to make it worth continuing. Some of them simply cannot
sustain the business.

So even if you have the most original idea for starting a new business
you should be highly sceptical about starting up a new enterprise. You
should get professional advice on the hurdles you face and the sources
of finance available. You may also need further training and you will
certainly need support from your family and friends. Make sure you
consult people who have embarked on similar or related projects
before.

If you are buying an existing business you must seek financial advice to
ensure that you are getting a good deal. You should get a qualified
accountant to go over the books to check that everything is above
board. Running a credit check on the company through a credit check
agency would also be a good idea. Obtaining any accounts filed with
the Corporate Affairs Commission or Companies House (a legal
requirement for limited companies in the UK) would also be necessary.
If no accounts have been filed, or they do not tally with the books, or
the accountant you have hired is wary of the company, it would
probably be advisable not to proceed with the purchase. Obtaining
legal advice from a solicitor on drawing up a contract is also a sensible
option.

You could also ask previous customers and acquaintances of the
company to verify their credibility and financial standing of the
company.

2. Do you want to move up, down or sideways on the career ladder?

Only you can really decide where you want to be on the career ladder, although some positions may be completely unrealistic. If you have been stuck in a rut and denied the promotion you feel you deserved, now is the time to aim high. Alternatively if you would like a less demanding job, now is the time to go for it. Obtaining a job that is similar to your current position is generally the easiest option.

3. What sort of company would you like to work for?

You will need to consider whether you want to work for a large, medium-sized or small company. What did you dislike in your current/previous jobs and what did you like? This will help you decide on which sort of companies you may want to approach.

Do you like to be someone who really counts in a small firm, or do you prefer to work in a large, established company? In a large company you may be a very small cog in a large wheel, whereas in a small firm you can have a greater influence and your actions might make a real difference to the fortunes of the firm.

Some people feel that large firms offer more job security, but these days large firms are making a lot of people redundant, so they cannot necessarily offer more job security than a smaller firm. Smaller firms tend to offer fewer fringe benefits than larger firms, but they may offer bigger bonuses.

The culture in a small firm tends to be more open and friendly, whilst large organizations can seem impersonal and unfriendly. A lot of large firms are trying to redress the balance, and many top executives can now be seen in the ordinary works canteen rather than in the executive canteen. Office politics tend to dominate more in a large firm although all firms have a certain amount of office politics.

If the size or culture of a firm is important to you, please ensure that any firm you apply to meets your criteria. It is often a good idea to talk to existing employees of the firm and always ask questions at an interview so you can deduce the good points and bad points about working at the firm.

4. Do you want to move into a different sector or industry?

You may want to consider moving into a different industry or a new sector of your current industry. This will be an important consideration if your current industry or sector is declining, or if jobs are hard to come by, or you just fancy a change.

5. Can you change profession or direction?
This may be the hardest question for you to answer if you are unsure about your current career path. You should take some time out to think about a radical change in your career as this may have major implications later on.

You should talk any major changes through with your family and dependants as this may have a significant impact on their lives, if it means a period studying (when you are not earning) or a period when you have to take a cut in salary to get on the first rung in your new profession.

You will need to gather as much information as possible on your new profession before making a final decision, including which qualifications are needed (if any), how you can study for the qualifications (full-time, part-time, evening courses, distance learning, etc), where you can study and how you can obtain relevant work experience. It is also a good idea to see if there are any work placements to give you a taste of the job (you do not want to study for something and then find you hate it!). Find out too what people in the profession think are the high points and low points of the job.

6. Which job could you do?
Only you can actually decide which job you want to do, but discussing your options with a career counsellor or a close friend or relative can assist you in making a decision. If you are considering a new career direction you should discuss this carefully with someone who has already followed this career path.

To help you decide on the options you face, it may be advantageous for you to write down all your options and score them as in the following example for a lawyer (10 is the top score and 1 is the bottom score).

Position	Interest	Knowledge	Experience
Employee Solicitor	5	9	9
Sole Practitioner	8	7	3
Associate Partner	9	2	1
Principal Partner	10	3	1

The Lawyer in our above example is only semi-interested in another similar position and would really like to progress to the position of sole practitioner. Other positions that are of interest are associate partner in an existing firm where he might buy equity shares or become a principal partner in a partnership. These positions are probably not very realistic at the moment without further training, experience and savings.

The same may apply to some of your own ideas and you will need a certain amount of determination if you want to pursue them. To start with you should talk to people in any profession you would like to join. Professional institutions or trade associations may also be prepared to offer advice. You will also need to find out if there are any openings in your area or whether you will have to move to a different location.

7. Are you too young or too old for the position?
It is necessary to consider your age while making a career choice. You might be too young or too old for the career you love. In some professions, there are minimum and maximum age limits. Being classed as too young or too old can often be a barrier to entering a new profession or indeed to just obtaining a new position. If you are not in the desired age range, what can you do?

It is important that you do not let yourself become disillusioned with your job search if you are the victim of ageism. You may have to investigate other routes of finding work and not rely only on advertised jobs. Look out for alternative plans and opportunities.

8. Do you want a job close to home or in another region or abroad?

Deciding on where you want to live will naturally affect the type and range of jobs on offer to you. You may want to work close to where you currently live, or you might want to move to another region, or you might want to work abroad. Only you (in consultation with your family if you have one) can decide where you want to live. Your choices may also be hampered by your current career, as there may not be any jobs in your current region or the region that you want to move to. If there are no jobs in your locality or you have exhausted all possibilities, you may have to look further afield or consider a change in career.

If you have a partner, or if you are the second wage earner in the household, your choices of geographical location may be very limited. You may need to consider retraining or a change in career if you cannot find anything suitable in your current area.

CHAPTER 12
6 STEPS TO A BUSINESS CHOICE

In case you decide to begin a business, that is not a bad idea, provided it is what you want to do. Choosing a business to start can be a difficult undertaking, especially if you have a lot of ideas, but just cannot make up your mind. But even if you have no idea about what business to start, you have to consider a number of factors in your decision-making process. Review the following list of steps as you choose a business to start.

1. Choose what you love.
Choose a business based on what you love doing. A business built upon a passion is usually more successful, because it allows you to do - on a regular basis - what you love. You will also be more enthusiastic about the business, determined to make sure it runs to your standards, and motivated to grow it. Your attitude will favorably impress any employees you may have, and your customers.

When I realised this, I decided to build my business around the things I love doing which are writing, speaking, mentoring, coaching and consulting. Life has been awesome since then. If your business is built around what you love, every day of business is a day of fun.

2. Consider your life style
Pick a business that fits into your current life or the life you wish to maintain. For example, you may have thought about starting your own real estate business, but the demands of this type of business may not be conducive to your family values. Typically, a real estate agent works all day and into the evening. If you have a family, you may not want to be away for so much of the day. There are many options for many scenarios, so consider them all and the kind of life you want to have, and make sure that they work together successfully.

If your faith demands that you should go to church every Sunday, you should not start a business that thrives best on Sundays. Such businesses like a beer parlour in an estate will demand that you do business on Sunday.

3. Leverage on previous knowledge, experience and network.

Build a business on what you already know and are good at. If you have been in sales all your life, and have done well, then choose a business that allows you to sell. If you have built relationships with people in a specific industry, then consider starting a business that allows you to take advantage of those contacts.

This would allow you to leverage on past experiences or old customer base. If you have served as a car sales agent, you may consider Car business when you want to start your own business.

4. Cut Your Business Coat According to Your Finances

Consider your financial status when comparing business opportunities. If you don't have the finances or the means to borrow the funds to start a particular business, then you may need to opt for a business that does not excessively rely on start-up cost. Your other option would be to wait until you can raise the money.

5. Let Your Business Solve a Problem

Think of a product or service in demand but currently under-provided. Research your community for ideas, or maybe you have been in need of a product or service but cannot get it easily. Choosing a business that offers a unique service or product will likely ensure your status in the market, assuming no competition moves in. Make sure that there is a big enough need for this service or product to keep your business profitable.

6. Consider a Franchise as a business idea, if Possible

Franchising is a business model in which many different owners share a single brand name. A parent company allows entrepreneurs to use the company's strategies and trademarks; in exchange, the franchisee pays an initial fee and royalties based on revenues. The parent company also provides the franchisee with support, including advertising and training, as part of the franchising agreement.

Additionally, franchises provide you with marketing materials and ideas to build customers. Remember, however, that when you get a franchise, you will be expected to meet certain expectations as far as policy and process are concerned.

CHAPTER 13
MORE QUOTES THAT MAY HELP

"My career should adapt to me. Fame is like a VIP pass wherever you want to go."

- Leonardo DiCaprio

"A career is born in public, talent in privacy."

- Marilyn Monroe

"The darkest day in a man's career is that wherein he fancies there is some easier way of getting a dollar than by squarely earning it."

- Horace Greeley

"The career of a writer is comparable to that of a woman of easy virtue. You write first for pleasure, later for the pleasure of others and finally for money."

- Marcel Achard

"Literature boils with the madcap careers of writers brought to the edge by the demands of living on their nerves, wringing out their memories and their nightmares to extract meaning, truth, and beauty."

- Herbert Gold

"If the career you have chosen has some unexpected inconvenience, console yourself by reflecting that no career is without them."

- Jane Fonda

"Job security is gone. The driving force of a career must come from the individual."

- Homa Bahrami

"Analyzing what you haven't got as well as what you have is a necessary ingredient of a career."

- Orison Swett Marden

"Many people worry so much about managing their careers, but rarely spend half that much energy managing their LIVES. I want to make my life, not just my job, the best it can be. The rest will work itself out."

- Reese Witherspoon

"The best careers advice to give to the young is 'Find out what you like doing best and get someone to pay you for doing it.'"

- Katherine Whitethorn

"One thing I know: the only ones among you who will be really happy are those who will have sought and found how to serve."

- Albert Schweitzer

"There is work that is work and there is play that is play; there is play that is work and work that is play. And in only one of these lie happiness."

- Gelett Burgess

"'But' is a fence over which few leap."

- German proverb

"I am an old man and have known a great many troubles, but most of them never happened."

- Mark Twain

"To play it safe is not to play."

- Robert Altman

"Heaven and hell is right now . . . You make it heaven, or you make it hell, by your actions."

- George Harrison

"Most folks are about as happy as they make up their minds to be."

- Abraham Lincoln

"We either make ourselves miserable, or we make ourselves strong. The amount of work is the same."

-Carlos Castaneda

"One can never consent to creep when one feels the impulse to soar."

- Helen Keller

"Let the world know you as you are, not as you think you should be, because sooner or later, if you are posing, you will forget the pose, and then where are you?"

- Fanny Brice

"The self is not something that one finds. It's something one creates."

- Thomas Szasz

"A bit of advice given to a young Native American at the time of his initiation: As you go the way of life, you will see a great chasm. Jump. It is not as wide as you think."

- Joseph Campbell

"The privilege of a lifetime is being who you are."

- Joseph Campbell

"Any human being is really good at certain things. The problem is that the things you're good at come naturally. And since most people are pretty modest instead of an arrogant s.o.b. like me, what comes naturally, you don't see as a special skill. It's just you. It's what you've always done."

- Stephen Jay Gould, evolutionary scientist

"Take someone who doesn't keep score, who's not looking to be richer, or afraid of losing, who has not the slightest interest even in his own personality: He's free."

- Rumi, poet born 1207 in Balkh (what is now Afghanistan)

"How strange is the lot of us mortals. Each of us is here for a brief sojourn; for what purpose he knows not, though he sometimes thinks he senses it. But without deeper reflection one knows from daily life that one exists for other people."

- Albert Einstein, 1931

"If you don't stand for something, you'll fall for anything."

- Michael Evans

"Unless a man has trained himself for his chance, the chance will only make him ridiculous."

- William Matthews

"I am seeking, I am striving, I am in it with all my heart."
                                                    - Vincent Van Gogh

"He who would learn to fly one day must first learn to stand and walk and run and climb and dance; one cannot fly into flying."
                                                    - Nietzsche

"I think and think for months, for years. Ninety-nine times the conclusion is false. The hundredth time I am right."
                                                    - Albert Einstein

"Remember, if you don't know where you're going, it doesn't matter how you get there."
                                                    - The Flying Karamazov Brothers

"You must be the change you wish to see in the world."
                                                    - Mohandas K. Gandhi

"We couldn't possibly know where it would lead, but we knew it had to be done."
                                    - Betty Friedan (pioneer of the Women's Movement)

"Dare to be naive."
- R. Buckminster Fuller (inventor & visionary for the most efficient use
                                    of Spaceship Earth's resources)

"Work and Play are words used to describe the same thing under different circumstances."
                                                    - Mark Twain

"Starting out to make money is the greatest mistake in life. Do what you feel you have a flair for doing, and if you are good enough at it, the money will come."
                                                    - Greer Garson

"To love what you do and feel that it matters--how could anything be more fun?"
                                                    - Katharine Graham

"I love Mickey Mouse more than any woman I've ever known."
                                                    - Walt Disney

"I went into the academic world under the illusion that it was a place where people cared passionately about ideas, about teaching, about discourse, about reflecting critically. What I discovered was a world of small-minded, partisan professionals, many of whom where there because they couldn't figure out what else to do. So I created a life inside the academy that reflected the life I wanted to lead."
- Benjamin R. Barber, author of "Jihad Vs McWorld"

"By believing passionately in something that does not yet exist, we create it. The non-existent is whatever we have not sufficiently desired."

- Nikos Kazantzakis

"I want my identity back. I don't want to be known as the CEO of AOL Time Warner . . . I'm my own person. I have strong moral convictions. I'm not just a suit. I want poetry back in my life."
- Gerald Levin, former CEO of AOL Time Warner
(the world's largest media company)

"Why change the world? To me that's what life is about. If you don't do that, you might as well hibernate and sleep. If everyone thinks what you do is 'normal' . . . it probably is. Why do that? Do something else!"
- Dean Kamen, Inventor of "Ginger,"
a personal transportation breakthrough

"Quite clearly nature did not tell the honeybee to go out and cross pollinate the vegetation. What nature did was to genetically program the honeybee to go after the honey and inadvertently cross-pollinate... What nature told humanity (genetically) was, I'm hungry, my kids are hungry; I'm cold, my kids are cold. Go after that food and coat. They cost money—go after the money. They say you have to earn it. OK, I'll earn it. Buzz, buzz, honey-money bee. No human genes are programmed to say 'go make the world work for everybody'—only your creative mind can tell you that."

- Buckminster Fuller

"We are given in our newspapers and on TV and radio exactly what we, the public, insist on having, and this very frequently is mediocre information and mediocre entertainment."

- Eleanor Roosevelt

"... [I have] a vision of a day when brains become as celebrated in America as brawn . . . that sports [will] remain merely as pastimes and that the world needs the smarts of young people to tackle larger problems. Clean water, clean air, health care, getting people out of ignorance and poverty - that's important."

- Dean Kamen, inventor
(as quoted in the Washington Post)

"Your work is to discover your work and then with all your heart to give yourself to it."

- Buddha

"I write lustily and humorously. It isn't calculated; it's the way I think. I've invented a writing style that expresses who I am."

- Erica Jong

"We don't see many fat men walking on stilts."

- Bud Miller

"If you go to heaven without being naturally talented for it, you will not enjoy it there."

- George Bernard Shaw

"I had all those cable networks reporting to me, I had a number of windows in my office and I had all the corporate perks you could possibly imagine, but that wasn't what I was about, so I left."

- Geraldine B. Laybourne, resigned as President of cable TV operations for ABC & Walt Disney Co., now with Oxygen Media

"You have to deal with the fact that your life is your life."

- Alex Hailey

"If you have to support yourself, you had bloody well better find some way that is going to be interesting."

- Katherine Hepburn

"A first-rate soup is better than a second-rate painting."

- Abraham Maslow

"I'm a salami writer. I try to write good salami, but salami is salami."

- Stephen King

"Different people have different duties assigned to them by nature; nature has given one the power or the desire to do this, the other that. Each bird must sing with his own throat."

- Anonymous

"The creation of something new is not accomplished by the intellect but by the play instinct acting from inner necessity. The creative mind plays with objects it loves."

- Carl G. Jung

"The people who get on in this world are the people who get up and look for the circumstances they want, and, if they can't find them, make them."

- George Bernard Shaw

"If people knew how hard I worked to get my mastery, it wouldn't seem so wonderful after all."

- Michelangelo

"A musician must make his music, an artist must paint, a poet must write if he is to ultimately be at peace with himself."

- Abraham Maslow

"Often people attempt to live their lives backwards: they try to have more things, or more money, in order to do more of what they want so that they will be happier. The way it actually works is the reverse. You must first be who you really are, then, do what you need to do, in order to have what you want."

- Margaret Young

"Far better it is to dare mighty things, to win glorious triumphs, even though checkered by failure, than to take rank with those poor spirits who neither enjoy much nor suffer much, because they live in the gray twilight that knows not victory nor defeat."

- Teddy Roosevelt

"Destiny is not a matter of chance. It is a matter of choice: it is not to be waited for, it is a thing to be achieved."

- William Jennings Bryan

"The supreme accomplishment is to blur the line between work and play."

- Arnold Toynbee

ABOUT THE T2D PROGRAM

Time to Decide Career & Business Choice Coaching Programme

Time to Decide programme is a Career-Choice Coaching package designed to empower individuals and groups to make the right career choices at the right time. The programme has been developed to ensure that participants get their career decisions right at the first go, basing their choice on who they are, what they love and the zeal to serve others with what they love and get paid for it.

The main objective of this programme is to empower the participants to find realistic, fulfilling, and enjoyable occupational options by identifying personality styles and matching that style to appropriate occupational choices.

Firstly, each participant embarks on a journey to discover who he or she is in the world they live in. All are empowered to discover that they are part of the world and that they are here for a purpose. This part of the programme awakens and unleashes the giant within as participants answer powerful, leading questions.

Secondly, they are led through a journey of self-evaluation. They are empowered to assess the life they are living. They are led to ask the question, "who am i?" This naturally leads on to who am i being? Why am i on this planet? What am i doing? What should i be doing? How am i doing it? How should i be doing it? What is there in life for me? What is next? This journey arouses in the participants the will for self-evaluation and assessment that enables them to revalue, rediscover and redefine themselves

Thirdly, each participant is led through the journey of self-assertion that empowers him or her to make a decision. As participants engage in the exercises, they are also empowered to explore available opportunities and make a choice. Using the results of self-discovery and self-evaluation, they are led through the self-assertion and decision-making process,

Finally, participants are guided through the career goal-setting process. They are empowered to harness their choices into achievable career goals and create action steps and plans to achieve them. They are led to organize these steps and plans with deadlines, and to create clear day-to-day steps that will lead to their career goals.

Those who complete the programme are encouraged to sign a commitment form. This is a formal document in which they affirm that they will remain focused and committed to their career goals until they become who they are.

The Benefits of the T2D Programme

Benefits to Participants

The first pay-off is the empowerment to make a career choice based on who they are, what they love and the zeal to serve others with what they love and get paid for it. This in turn leads to financial freedom, benefit to the community, and happy living with less effort.

- Participants become more self-conscious and begin to appreciate themselves more.
- Increases productivity efficiency and reduces stress.
- Participants discover special skills that they can get paid for.
- They become more motivated and learn to take complete charge of their lives.
- By the end of the programme, their self-image, self-esteem and self-confidence explode!
- They become like mighty rivers, more focused, more directed and more channeled, moving forward over all obstacles and barriers to their career goals.
- Most importantly, the world will be better place because the individuals end up being happy, financially free and of benefit to the entire community in whatever career they choose.

Benefits to the Community

- Young people are empowered to focus on their goals. They become busy with their action plans and as a result have no time for loitering, violence, cults and gangs.
- Without the right career choices, academic learning loses its purpose.
- Undecided individuals often lose their motivation to endure through academic and school struggles.
- People will be more passionate with their careers and not motivated by just money and prestige, thus reducing corruption.
- In the long run, the work force will be full of motivated people.

- People will become more engaged in what they do.
- Job-applicants will become more specialized and suitable for their roles.
- Most people will become happy with their jobs.
- Workers will be more productive and the entire community will benefit.

BE YOURSELF

Why would you want to be someone else?
When you can be better being yourself
Why pretend to be someone you are not?
When you have something they haven't got

Cheating yourself of the life you have to live
Deprives others of that which only you can give.
You have much more to offer by being just you
Than walking around in someone else's shoes.

Trying to live the life of another is a mistake
It is a masquerade; nothing more than a fake
Be yourself and let your qualities show through
Others will love you more, for being just you

Remember that God loves you just as you are
To Him you are already a bright shining star
Family and friends will love you more too
If you spend time practicing just being

Ellen Bailey

Other Relevant Books by Chigbo Ugwuoke:

1. **Time for Action:** *15 Strategic Skills for Workplace Efficiency, Effectiveness & Productivity.*
2. **Time to Excel**: *15 Golden Steps to The Career Top.*
3. **Time for Jobsearch 1**: *10 Secrets and Strategies for Winning the CV Game.*
4. **Time for Jobsearch 2**: *10 Smart Tips for Mastering Job Interviews.*
5. **Jobsearch 101:** *One Hundred and One Mistakes Jobseekers Make & How You Can Avoid Them.*
6. **Top 10 Mistakes Parents Make While Helping Their Children Choose Secondary School Subjects & University Degrees;** *Their effects & How You Can Avoid Them*

www.ingramcontent.com/pod-product-compliance
Lightning Source LLC
Chambersburg PA
CBHW020606030426
42337CB00013B/1237